XAMonline, Inc.
25 First Street, Suite 106
Cambridge, MA 02141
Toll Free: 1-800-509-4128
Email: info@xamonline.com
Web: www.xamonline.com
Fax: 1-617-583-5552

Library of Congress Cataloging-in-Publication Data

Wynne, Sharon A.
    PRAXIS Elementary Education 0011, 0012 Practice Test 1: Teacher Certification /
    Sharon A. Wynne. -1st ed.
    ISBN: 978-1-60787-117-0
    1. PRAXIS Elementary Education 0011, 0012 Practice Test 1   2. Study Guides
    3. PRAXIS   4. Teachers' Certification & Licensure   5. Careers

Disclaimer:

The opinions expressed in this publication are the sole works of XAMonline and were created independently from the National Education Association, Educational Testing Service, or any State Department of Education, National Evaluation Systems or other testing affiliates.

Between the time of publication and printing, state specific standards as well as testing formats and website information may change that is not included in part or in whole within this product. Sample test questions are developed by XAMonline and reflect similar content as on real tests; however, they are not former tests. XAMonline assembles content that aligns with state standards but makes no claims nor guarantees teacher candidates a passing score. Numerical scores are determined by testing companies such as NES or ETS and then are compared with individual state standards. A passing score varies from state to state.

Printed in the United States of America   œ-1
PRAXIS Elementary Education 0011, 0012 Practice Test 1
ISBN: 978-1-60787-117-0

READING

1. **All of the following are true about phonological awareness EXCEPT:** *(Average) (Skill 1.2, 2.1)*

    A. It may involve print.

    B. It is a prerequisite for spelling and phonics.

    C. Activities can be done by the children with their eyes closed.

    D. Starts before letter recognition is taught.

2. **The arrangement and relationship of words in sentences or sentence structure best describes:** *(Average) (Skill 1.3)*

    A. Style

    B. Discourse

    C. Thesis

    D. Syntax

3. **Which of the following indicates that a student is a fluent reader?** *(Average) (Skill 1.3)*

    A. Reads texts with expression or prosody

    B. Reads word-to-word and haltingly

    C. Must intentionally decode a majority of the words

    D. In a writing assignment, sentences are poorly organized, structurally

4. **Which of the following reading strategies is NOT associated with fluent reading abilities?** *(Rigorous) (Skill 1.3)*

    A. Pronouncing unfamiliar words by finding similarities with familiar words

    B. Establishing a purpose for reading

    C. Formulating questions about the text while reading

    D. Reading sentences word by word

5. **Orthography is:**
   (Rigorous) (Skill 1.3)

   A. The study of word structure

   B. A method of representing a spoken language through the use of written symbols

   C. The complete set of related word-forms associated with a given lexeme

   D. A process of word-formation that involves combining complete word-forms into a single compound form

6. **Which word in the following sentence is a bound morpheme? "The quick brown fox jumped over the lazy dog"**
   (Rigorous) (Skill 1.4)

   A. The

   B. fox

   C. lazy

   D. jumped

7. **Which of the following reading strategies calls for higher order cognitive skills?**
   (Average) (Skill 1.5)

   A. Making predictions

   B. Summarizing

   C. Monitoring

   D. Making inferences

8. **Answering questions, monitoring comprehension, and interacting with a text are common methods of:**
   (Average) (Skill 1.5)

   A. Whole-class instruction

   B. Comprehension instruction

   C. Research-based instruction

   D. Evidence-based instruction

9. **Mrs. Young is a first grade teacher trying to select a books that are "just right" for her students to read independently. She needs to consider which of the following:**
   (Rigorous) (Skill 1.5)

   A. Illustrations should support the meaning of the text

   B. Content that relates to student interest and experiences

   C. Predictable text structures and language patterns

   D. All of the above

10. **Which of the following is NOT a characteristic of a fable?**
(Easy) (Skill 1.6)

  A. Animals that feel and talk like humans

  B. Happy solutions to human dilemmas

  C. Teaches a moral or standard for behavior

  D. Illustrates specific people or groups without directly naming them

11. **The children's literature genre came into its own in the:**
(Average) (Skill 1.6)

  A. Seventeenth century

  B. Eighteenth century

  C. Nineteenth century

  D. Twentieth century

12. **Which of the following is NOT characteristic of a folktale?**
(Average) (Skill 1.6)

  A. Considered true among various societies

  B. A hero on a quest

  C. Good versus evil

  D. Adventures of animals

13. **In her kindergarten class, Mrs. Thomas has been watching the students in the drama center. She has watched the children pretend to complete a variety of magic tricks. Mrs. Thomas decides to use stories about magic to share with her class. Her decision to incorporate their interests into the reading shows that Mrs. Thomas understands that:**
(Average) (Skill 1.6)

  A. Including student interests is important at all times

  B. Teaching by themes is crucial for young children

  C. Young children respond to literature that reflects their lives

  D. Science fiction and fantasy are the most popular genres

14. **Which is an untrue statement about a theme in literature?**
(Rigorous) (Skill 1.7)

  A. The theme is always stated directly somewhere in the text

  B. The theme is the central idea in a literary work

  C. All parts of the work (plot, setting, mood should contribute to the theme in some way

  D. By analyzing the various elements of the work, the reader should be able to arrive at an indirectly stated theme

15. Which of the following is an opinion?
(Easy) (Skill 1.7)

A. The sky is blue

B. Albany is the capital of New York State

C. A dog is the best pet to have

D. Humans breathe

16. Which is NOT a true statement concerning an author's literary tone?
(Rigorous) (Skill 1.7)

A. Tone is partly revealed through the selection of details

B. Tone is the expression of the author's attitude toward his/her subject

C. Tone in literature is usually satiric or angry

D. Tone in literature corresponds to the tone of voice a speaker uses

17. Which of the following is an example of nonfiction literature?
(Average) (Skill 1.7)

A. Letters

B. Biographies

C. Journals

D. All of the above

18. A student has written a paper with the following characteristics: written in first person; characters, setting, and plot; some dialogue; events organized in chronological sequence with some flashbacks. In what genre has the student written?
(Easy) (Skill 1.7)

A. Expository writing

B. Narrative writing

C. Persuasive writing

D. Technical writing

19. Which of the following is important in understanding fiction?
(Rigorous) (Skill 1.7)

I. Realizing the artistry in telling a story to convey a point.
II. Knowing fiction is imaginary.
III. Seeing what is truth and what is perspective.
IV. Acknowledging the difference between opinion and truth.

A. I and II only

B. II and IV only

C. III and IV only

D. IV only

20. **All of the following are correctly capitalized EXCEPT:**
(Average) (Skill 1.8)

A. Queen Elizabeth

B. Congressman McKay

C. Commander Alger

D. The President of the United States

21. **All of the following are correctly punctuated EXCEPT:**
(Rigorous) (Skill 1.8)

A. "The book is on the table," said Bill's mother.

B. "Who would like to sing 'The Star Spangled Banner'?" the teacher asked.

C. I was embarrassed when Joanne said, "The meeting started an hour ago!"

D. "The policeman apprehended the criminals last night."

22. **Which of the following sentences contains a subject-verb agreement error?**
(Average) (Skill 1.8)

A. Both mother and her two sisters were married in a triple ceremony.

B. Neither the hen nor the rooster is likely to be served for dinner.

C. My boss, as well as the company's two personnel directors, have been to Spain.

D. Amanda and the twins are late again.

23. **Which of the following are punctuated correctly?** *(Rigorous) (Skill 1.8)*

   I.   **The teacher directed us to compare Faulkner's three symbolic novels Absalom, Absalom; As I Lay Dying; and Light in August.**
   II. **Three of Faulkner's symbolic novels are: Absalom, Absalom; As I Lay Dying; and Light in August.**
   III. **The teacher directed us to compare Faulkner's three symbolic novels: Absalom, Absalom; As I Lay Dying; and Light in August.**
   IV. **Three of Faulkner's symbolic novels are Absalom, Absalom; As I Lay Dying; and Light in August.**

   A. I and II only

   B. II and III only

   C. III and IV only

   D. IV only

24. **If a student uses inappropriate language that includes slang and expletives, what is the best course of action to take in order to influence the student's formal communication skills?** *(Rigorous) (Skill 1.10)*

   A. Ask the student to paraphrase the writing, that is, translate it into language appropriate for the school principal to read

   B. Refuse to read the student's papers until he conforms to a more literate style

   C. Ask the student to read his work aloud to the class for peer evaluation

   D. Rewrite the flagrant passages to show the student the right form of expression

25. **Which of the following is an example of alliteration?** *(Average) (Skill 2.1)*

   A. "The City's voice itself is soft like Solitude."

   B. "Both in one faith unanimous; though sad"

   C. "By all their country's wishes blest!"

   D. "In earliest Greece to these with partial choice."

26. **According to Marilyn Jager Adams, which skill would a student demonstrate by identifying that cat does not belong in the group of words containing dog, deer, and dress?**
(Average) (Skill 2.1)

A. Recognize the odd member in a group

B. Replace sounds in words

C. Count the sounds in a word

D. Count syllables in a word

27. **Which of the following is NOT a characteristic of a good reader?**
(Rigorous) (Skill 2.4)

A. When faced with unfamiliar words, they skip over them unless meaning is lost

B. They formulate questions that they predict will be answered in the text

C. They establish a purpose before reading

D. They go back to reread when something doesn't make sense

28. **Which of the following is NOT a strategy of teaching reading comprehension?**
(Rigorous) (Skill 2.5)

A. Summarization

B. Utilizing graphic organizers

C. Manipulating sounds

D. Having students generate questions

29. **Which of the following is NOT a technique of prewriting?**
(Average) (Skill 2.6)

A. Clustering

B. Listing

C. Brainstorming

D. Proofreading

30. **Which of the following is NOT an approach to keep students ever conscious of the need to write for audience appeal?**
(Rigorous) (Skill 2.6)

    A. Pairing students during the writing process

    B. Reading all rough drafts before the students write the final copies

    C. Having students compose stories or articles for publication in school literary magazines or newspapers

    D. Writing letters to friends or relatives

31. **Which of the following mostly addresses grammatical and technical errors?**
(Easy) (Skill 2.6)

    A. Revising

    B. Editing

    C. Proofreading

    D. Rough draft writing

32. **All of the following are stages of the writing process EXCEPT:**
(Average) (Skill 2.6)

    A. Prewriting

    B. Revising

    C. Organizing

    D. Presenting

33. **Which of the following is true about semantics?**
(Average) (Skill 2.7)

    A. Semantics will sharpen the effect and meaning of a text

    B. Semantics refers to the meaning expressed when words are arranged in a specific way

    C. Semantics is a vocabulary instruction technique

    D. Semantics is representing spoken language through the use of symbols

34. **Jose moved to the United States last month. He speaks little or no English at this time. His teacher is teaching the class about habitats in science and has chosen to read a story about various habitats to the class. The vocabulary is difficult. What should Jose's teacher do with Jose?**
(Rigorous) (Skill 2.7)

    A. Provide Jose with additional opportunities to learn about habitats

    B. Read the story to Jose multiple times

    C. Show Jose pictures of habitats from his native country

    D. Excuse Jose from the assignment

35. John is having difficulty reading the word reach. In isolation, he pronounces each sound as /r/ /ee/ /sh/. Which of the following is a possible instructional technique that could help solve John's reading difficulty?
(Rigorous) (Skill 3.1)

A. Additional phonemic awareness instruction

B. Additional phonics instruction

C. Additional skill and drill practice

D. Additional minimal pair practice

36. To decode is to:
(Easy) (Skill 3.2)

A. Construct meaning

B. Sound out a printed sequence of letters

C. Use a special code to decipher a message

D. None of the above

37. Which of the following is a formal reading level assessment?
(Easy) (Skill 3.2)

A. A standardized reading test

B. A teacher-made reading test

C. An interview

D. A reading diary

38. Which of the following is NOT one of the metalinguistic abilities acquired by children from early involvement in reading activities?
(Rigorous) (Skill 3.3)

A. Conventions of print

B. Word consciousness

C. Spelling fluency

D. Functions of print

39. The English department is developing strategies to encourage all students to become a community of readers. From the list of suggestions below, which would be the least effective way for teachers to foster independent reading?
(Average) (Skill 3.3)

A. Each teacher will set aside a weekly 30-minute in-class reading session during which the teacher and students read a magazine or book for enjoyment

B. Teacher and students develop a list of favorite books to share with each other

C. The teacher assigns at least one book report each grading period to ensure that students are reading from the established class list

D. The students gather books for a classroom library so that books may be shared with each other

40. **As Ms. Wolmark looks at the mandated vocabulary curriculum for the 5th grade, she notes that she can opt to teach foreign words and abbreviations, which have become part of the English language. She decides:**
(Rigorous) (Skill 3.3)

   A. To forego that since she is not a teacher of foreign language

   B. To teach only foreign words from the native language of her four ELL students

   C. To use the ELL students' native languages as a start for an extensive study of foreign language words

   D. To teach 2 or 3 foreign language words that are now in English and let it go at that

41. **Which of the following is a convention of print that children learn during reading activities?**
(Average) (Skill 3.3)

   A. The meaning of words

   B. The left to right motion

   C. The purpose of print

   D. The identification of letters

42. **Reading a piece of student writing to assess the overall impression of the product is**
(Average) (Skill 3.7)

   A. Holistic evaluation

   B. Portfolio assessment

   C. Analytical evaluation

   D. Using a performance system

READING ESSAYS

Sean is five years old and in kindergarten. He is precocious and seems to have a lot of energy throughout the day. Sean has a hard time settling down in the classroom, and the teacher often needs to redirect him in order to have him complete assignments. Sean is struggling in many areas, but currently his lowest area is in writing. Though it is January, Sean still does not seem to be making the appropriate sound symbol connection to make progress with his writing. Sean still needs to be reminded to use a tripod grasp on his pencil and often slips into a fist grip. His drawings are rushed and lack detail but are recognizable. Sean has made some progress with his skills though. At the beginning of the year, he was unable to make any recognizable letters. Now he always makes letters when he is writing; however, there are rarely spaces between the letters. Sean's progress in this area is significantly behind his peers, and you have decided to design an intervention plan to address these concerns.

How would you prioritize the areas where Sean is struggling within your intervention plan and provide justification as to why you would prioritize them in this manner? What instructional activities would you implement as part of the intervention plan? Finally, where else could you seek support and ideas for things to help address Sean's writing skills?

MATHEMATICS

1. **Preschool children are learning to count by teaching them a song. What method are you using?**
   (Easy) (Skill 4.1)

   A. Rote counting

   B. Guessing

   C. Memory

   D. Cite counting

2. **You are teaching a lesson on converting a decimal to a percent. How do you explain to students how to change a decimal to a percent?**
   (Average) (Skill 4.1)

   A. Divide by 100 or move the decimal point 2 places to the left

   B. Write the decimal as a fraction and then divided the numerator by the denominator

   C. Multiply the decimal by 100 or move the decimal point 2 places to the right

   D. Add a percent symbol

3. **The mathematical statement illustrates what property.**
   (Rigorous) (Skill 4.1)

   $a \bullet 1 = a$

   A. Inverse property of multiplication

   B. Identity property of multiplication

   C. Commutative property of multiplication

   D. Associative property of multiplication

4. **Which operation is used to solve the following application problem:**
   (Average) (Skill 4.1)

   You are hosting a surprise anniversary party. You plan to invite 145 people. The cost of mailing a letter or card $0.44. How much will it cost to send the invitations?

   A. Addition

   B. Subtraction

   C. Division

   D. Multiplication

5. **You give your pre-school students this problem. What level of mathematics are you beginning to teach your students?**
(Average) (Skill 4.2)

State the missing figure in the pattern.

A. Geometry

B. Pre-algebra and Algebra

C. Trigonometry

D. Basic Math

6. **Name the triangle.**
(Easy) (Skill 4.3)

A. Right triangle

B. Acute triangle

C. Equilateral triangle

D. Isosceles triangle

7. **What characteristic classifies a polygon as regular?**
(Rigorous) (Skill 4.3)

A. All sides have the same length and all angles have the same measure

B. All angles have the same measure

C. All sides are of different length, and all angle measures are different

D. All sides are the same length

8. The following definition describes what type of figure. Give an example of the figure.
    (Rigorous)(Skill 4.3)

    The union of all points on a simple closed surface and all points in its interior forms a space figure.

    A. Solid; rectangle

    B. Solid; sphere

    C. Polyhedra; cone

    D. Polygon; sphere

9. The following tessellation uses what type of transformational symmetry?
    (Average) (Skill 4.3)

    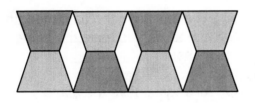

    A. Rotation

    B. Translation

    C. Glide reflection

    D. Rotation and translation

10. Measures in pound and kilograms describe what type of measurement?
    (Easy) (Skill 4.3)

    A. Temperature

    B. Weight

    C. Liquid volume

    D. Distance and area

11. Find the mean, standard deviation, and variance of the test scores. Use a calculator.
    (Average) (Skill 4.4)

    90, 75, 60, 90, 85

    A. Mean: 80, standard deviation: 12.74754878, variance: 162.5

    B. Mean: 12.74754878, standard deviation: 80, variance: 162.5

    C. Mean: 80, standard deviation: 162.5, variance: 12.74754878

    D. Mean: 90, standard deviation: 162.5 variance: 80

12. You are teaching a class of first graders how to add and subtract. Which of the follow manipulatives are not useful in teaching these skills?
(Average) (Skill 5.1)

A. Number lines

B. Algebra tiles

C. Counters

D. Jelly beans, raisins, chocolate chips, etc.

13. You would like to teach your students that math is important in their lives. Which activity listed below would not be a good activity for your student to do to show them math in their everyday lives?
(Rigorous) (Skill 5.1)

A. Research a mathematician

B. Design a playground

C. Bake a batch of cookies and measure the ingredients

D. Chart the weather on a daily basis

14. Your students were assigned a cross-curricular activity, math and social studies One of your students compared the rainfall amounts, for one year, of the United States and China. What type of display would not display the data in a meaningful way?
(Rigorous) (Skill 5.1)

A. Line graph

B. Bar chart

C. Circle graph

D. Table

15. You are introducing a unit on measurement to your second graders. You want to start with a fun activity to engage your students. Which of the following activities could you use?
(Average) (Skill 5.1)

A. Talk about distance using a map

B. Begin by discussing the Customary and Metric measurement systems

C. Talk about distance by using a replica of the solar system

D. Have students bring in a shoe from home; ask them to measure the distance from wall-to-wall using the shoe; then discuss the different amount of shoe lengths student get

16. Problem solving spans across the curriculum. In math, problem solving is usually presented in the form of "word problems" or real world applications. What is the first step you teach your students in problem solving?
(Easy) (Skill 5.2)

A. Understand the problem

B. Devise a plan

C. Carry out the plan

D. Look back

17. How would you teach your students to solve this problem?
(Average) (Skill 5.2)

The scale on a map is 1 inch = 50 miles. How many miles are there in 7 inches?

A. Pick a point on a map and draw a circle with a diameter of 7 inches

B. Use a map with the same scale and measure 7 inches

C. Use a proportion

D. Use estimation

18. You are teaching your students to solve problems involving percents. When working with percents, what must you tell your students to do to the percent before it can be used in solving a problem?
(Easy) (Skill 5.2)

A. Change the percent to a whole number

B. Do not change anything

C. Drop the percent symbol

D. Change the percent to a decimal

19. Why are manipulatives useful in teaching mathematics?
(Rigorous) (Skill 5.3)

A. Manipulatives make math fun.

B. Allow students to understand mathematical concepts by allowing them to see concrete examples of abstract processes.

C. Give the teacher a change of pace with instruction

D. Students like playing with them

20. **Technology is becoming helpful in teaching math. Which answer does not explain why?**
(Rigorous) (Skill 5.3)

A. Students have been using technology and playing video games before they were enrolled in school, making them very adept at using computers

B. Technology can be used to give individualized help to each student

C. Using technology gives the teacher a break from teaching

D. With technology programs, students can learn at their own pace and gain confidence in their ability to do math

21. **Why is planning some formal assessment during a lesson important?**
(Average) (Skill 6.1)

A. It gives the teacher a break from teaching

B. It allows students a chance to catch up on the material if they are behind

C. It allows the teacher to make sure all students understand the material; if they are not, it allows the teacher an opportunity to adjust the instruction

D. It's not a good idea to use formal assessment during a lesson

22. **Observation is the most effective method used when problem solving. Which answer is not an example of an activity in which a teacher can observe students to be sure they are understanding the material.**
(Rigorous) (Skill 6.2)

A. Watch students taking a test

B. Plan a cooperative activity for you students

C. Plan a game for the students that involves the math concepts you are teaching

D. Divide the class into groups, give each group a problem to solve where each student of the group must do a part of the problem

MATH ESSAYS

You have designed an alternative assessment based on a portfolio, observation, and oral presentation for a student with learning disabilities in the area of reading and writing. Your colleague is concerned that this lowers expectations for the student, deprives him of the chance to practice taking the kind of tests he needs to be successful and sets him further apart from the other students.

Justify your choice of an alternative assessment for the learning-disabled student in place of the traditional tests that other students are taking. How would you respond to your colleague's concerns and reassure her that the assessment you are planning is valid and in the best interests of the student?

SCIENCE

1. **What does a primary consumer most commonly refer to?**
    (Average) (Skill 7.1)

    A. Herbivore

    B. Autotroph

    C. Carnivore

    D. Decomposer

2. **All of the following are oceans EXCEPT:**
    (Easy) (Skill 7.2)

    A. Pacific

    B. Atlantic

    C. Mediterranean

    D. Indian

3. **What type of rock can be classified by the size of the crystals in the rock?**
    (Easy) (Skill 7.2)

    A. Metamorphic

    B. Igneous

    C. Minerals

    D. Sedimentary

4. **What are solids with a definite chemical composition and a tendency to split along planes of weakness?**
    (Easy) (Skill 7.2)

    A. Ores

    B. Rocks

    C. Minerals

    D. Salts

5. **What is a large, rotating, low-pressure system accompanied by heavy precipitation and strong winds known as?**
    (Easy) (Skill 7.2)

    A. A hurricane

    B. A tornado

    C. A thunderstorm

    D. A tsunami

6. **The breakdown of rock due to acid rain is an example of:**
    (Rigorous) (Skill 7.2)

    A. Physical weathering

    B. Frost wedging

    C. Chemical weathering

    D. Deposition

7. **The most abundant gas in the atmosphere is:**
   (Rigorous) (Skill 7.2)

   A. Oxygen

   B. Nitrogen

   C. Carbon dioxide

   D. Methane

8. **Which of the following is an example of a chemical change?**
   (Rigorous) (Skill 7.3)

   A. Freezing food to preserve it

   B. Using baking powder in biscuits

   C. Melting glass to make a vase

   D. Mixing concrete with water

9. **The main source of glucose in the human diet is:**
   (Average) (Skill 7.4)

   A. Carbohydrates

   B. Fat

   C. Protein

   D. Most forms of food

10. **Which scientist is credited with launching the Scientific Revolution in the 16th century?**
    (Rigorous) (Skill 8.1)

    A. Roger Bacon

    B. Nicolaus Copernicus

    C. Johannes Kepler

    D. Isaac Newton

11. **An experiment is performed to determine the effects of acid rain on plant life. Which of the following would be the variable?**
    (Average) (Skill 8.2)

    A. The type of plant

    B. The amount of light

    C. The ph of the water

    D. The amount of water

12. **What is the last step in the scientific method?**
    (Easy) (Skill 8.2)

    A. Pose a question

    B. Draw a conclusion

    C. Conduct a test

    D. Record data

13. An experiment is performed to determine how the surface area of a liquid affects how long it takes for the liquid to evaporate. One hundred milliliters of water is put in containers with surface areas of 10 cm², 30 cm², 50 cm², 70 cm², and 90 cm². The time it took for each container to evaporate is recorded. Which of the following is a controlled variable?
(Rigorous) (Skill 8.2)

A. The time required for each evaporation

B. The area of the surfaces

C. The amount of water

D. The temperature of the water

SCIENCE ESSAYS

A mechanical wave is a disturbance in a medium in which energy is propagated, but not bulk matter. Waves can be transverse or longitudinal. A wave has frequency, amplitude, and wavelength. The speed of a wave is determined by the medium.

What would be the instructional objective, lesson motivation, and student activity in a lesson about waves?

SOCIAL SCIENCES

1. **Which of the following is not one of the three main concepts of human-environment interaction?**
   (Easy) (Skill 10.1)

   A. Adapt

   B. Modify

   C. Depend

   D. Expand

2. **The Southern Hemisphere contains all of the following?**
   (Average) (Skill 10.1)

   A. Africa

   B. Australia

   C. South America

   D. North America

3. **What is the largest ocean on the planet?**
   (Easy) (Skill 10.1)

   A. Indian Ocean

   B. Pacific Ocean

   C. Atlantic Ocean

   D. Arctic Ocean

4. **Which best describes social history?**
   (Rigorous) (Skill 10.2)

   A. The study of ancient texts

   B. The study of politics of the past

   C. The study of societies of the past

   D. The study of history from a global perspective

5. **Which of the following is a weakness of "periodization"?**
   (Average) (Skill 10.2)

   A. It is arbitrary

   B. Facilitates understanding

   C. Identifies similarities

   D. Categorizes knowledge

6. **Which of the following are US citizens guaranteed?**
   (Easy) (Skill 10.3)

   A. Employment

   B. Post-Secondary Education

   C. Driver's License

   D. Free Speech

7. Which of the following is not a right declared by the US Constitution?
(Average) (Skill 10.3)

A. The right to speak out in public

B. The right to use cruel and unusual punishment

C. The right to a speedy trial

D. The right not to be forced to testify against yourself

8. What group is most responsible for enforcing the law?
(Average) (Skill 10.3)

A. Executive Branch

B. Individual States

C. Judicial Branch

D. Legislative Branch

9. Linguistics is which of the following?
(Average) (Skill 10.4)

A. Norms, values, standards

B. Study of material remains of humans

C. Genetic characteristics

D. The historical development of language

10. Which of the following refers to cultural influences?
(Average) (Skill 10.4)

A. General social patterns of groups of people in an area

B. Changes in attitudes, morale, and leadership

C. Organized groups of people

D. Wars, revolutions, inventions, and fashions

11. Which of the following can be considered the primary goal of social studies?
(Average) (Skill 10.5)

A. Recalling specific dates and places

B. Identifying and analyzing social links

C. Using contextual clues to identify eras

D. Linking experiments with history

SOCIAL SCIENCES ESSAYS

You are an elementary school teacher at a Title 1 school. Your school district has been unable to purchase new textbooks for your school in several years. Because of that, the Social Studies textbooks in your classroom are becoming quickly out-dated and there are no supplemental materials to use for hands-on learning. Along with teaching the content Social Studies standards, you also have to be sure that your students are learning Historical and Social Science Analysis Skills, which are often overlooked because of a lack of resources. These skills are not only an important aspect of creating independent thinkers in your classroom, they are also important to making Social Studies come alive for the students, to becoming relevant in their own lives. Being that you only have older Social Studies textbooks at your disposal and no additional resources in the classroom, you have to think "out of the box" to teach these analysis skills to your students.

Historical and Social Science Analysis Skills for grades K-5 include such ideas as:
- Chronological and Spatial Thinking
  - interpreting time lines
  - using terms related to time
  - connections between past and present
  - interpretation of maps and globes, and significance of location
- Research, Evidence, and Point of View
  - differentiation between primary and secondary sources
  - posing relevant questions about events and sources
  - distinguishing between fact and fiction
- Historical Interpretation
  - summarize key events and explain historical context of those events
  - identify human and physical characteristics of places and explain how these are unique to such places
  - identify and interpret multiple causes and effects of events

Given the above information and circumstance, create instructional strategies/activities to teach 2 to 3 of the Historical and Social Science Analysis Skills outlined above. These skills can be taught using any Social Studies content and are for grades K-5 as noted above.

ARTS

1. A student art sample book would include cotton balls and sandpaper to represent:
(Average) (Skill 13.1)

   A. Color

   B. Lines

   C. Texture

   D. Shape

2. Which terms refers to the arrangement of one or more items so they appear symmetrical or asymmetrical?
(Rigorous) (Skill 13.1)

   A. Balance

   B. Contrast

   C. Emphasis

   D. Unity

3. Sound waves are produced by _____.
(Easy) (Skill 13.2)

   A. pitch

   B. noise

   C. vibrations

   D. sonar

4. Common percussion instruments include:
(Average) (Skill 13.2)

   A. Xylophone, tambourine, and bells

   B. Trumpet, trombone, and tuba

   C. Oboe, clarinet, and saxophone

   D. Viola, cello, and piano

5. A combination of three or more tones sounded at the same time is called a:
(Average) (Skill 13.2)

   A. Harmony

   B. Consonance

   C. Chord

   D. Dissonance

6. A series of single tones which add up to a recognizable sound is called a:
(Average) (Skill 13.2)

   A. Cadence

   B. Rhythm

   C. Melody

   D. Sequence

7. The quality of sound is the definition of:
(Average) (Skill 13.2)

   A. Timbre

   B. Rhythm

   C. Harmony

   D. Melody

8. In visual arts such as music and dance, the intentional, regular repetition of a given element most commonly serves as a feeling of:
(Average) (14.1)

   A. Rhythm

   B. Dissonance

   C. Contrast

   D. Dominance

9. In visual art studies students are expected to be able to interact in all of the following exercises EXCEPT one.
(Average) (Skill 14.1)

   A. Clap out rhythmic patterns found in music lyrics

   B. Compare and contrast various art pieces

   C. Recognize related dance vocabulary

   D. Identify and sort pictures organized by shape, size, and color

10. Creating movements in response to music helps students to connect music and dance in which of the following ways?
(Average) (Skill 14.1)

    A. Rhythm

    B. Costuming

    C. Speed

    D. Vocabulary skills

11. Which subject would a color wheel most likely be used for?
(Easy) (Skill 14.1)

    A. Visual arts

    B. Music

    C. Movement

    D. Drama

12. What would watching a dance company performance be most likely to promote?
(Easy) (Skill 14.1)

    A. Critical thinking skills

    B. Appreciation of the arts

    C. Improvisation skills

    D. Music vocabulary

READING

1. **All of the following are true about phonological awareness EXCEPT:**
    (Average) (Skill 1.2, 2.1)

    A.   It may involve print

    B.   It is a prerequisite for spelling and phonics

    C.   Activities can be done by the children with their eyes closed

    D.   Starts before letter recognition is taught

Answer: A. It may involve print
The key word here is "except" which will be highlighted in upper case on the test as well. All of the options are correct aspects of phonological awareness except the first one, choice A, because phonological awareness does not involve print.

2. **The arrangement and relationship of words in sentences or sentence structure best describes:**
    (Average) (Skill 1.3)

    A.   Style

    B.   Discourse

    C.   Thesis

    D.   Syntax

Answer: D. Syntax
Syntax is the grammatical structure of sentences.

3. **Which of the following indicates that a student is a fluent reader?**
   (Average) (Skill 1.3)

   A.   Reads texts with expression or prosody

   B.   Reads word-to-word and haltingly

   C.   Must intentionally decode a majority of the words

   D.   In a writing assignment, sentences are poorly organized, structurally

Answer: A: Reads texts with expression or prosody.
The teacher should listen to the children read aloud, but there are also clues to reading levels in their writing.

4. **Which of the following reading strategies is NOT associated with fluent reading abilities?**
   (Rigorous) (Skill 1.3)

   A.   Pronouncing unfamiliar words by finding similarities with familiar words.

   B.   Establishing a purpose for reading.

   C.   Formulating questions about the text while reading.

   D.   Reading sentences word by word.

Answer: D. Reading sentences word by word
Pronouncing unfamiliar words by finding similarities with familiar words, establishing a purpose for reading, and formulating questions about the text while reading are all excellent strategies fluent readers use to enhance their comprehension of a text. Reading sentences word by word is a trait of a non-fluent reader as it inhibits comprehension as the reader is focused on each word by itself rather than the meaning of the whole sentence and how it fits into the text.

5. **Orthography is:**
   (Rigorous) (Skill 1.3)

   A.   The study of word structure

   B.   A method of representing a spoken language through the use of written symbols

   C.   The complete set of related word-forms associated with a given lexeme

   D.   A process of word-formation that involves combining complete word-forms into a single compound form

Answer: B. A method of representing a spoken language through the use of written symbols
By definition, orthography is using written symbols to represent spoken language.

6. **Which word in the following sentence is a bound morpheme?**
   "The quick brown fox jumped over the lazy dog"
   (Rigorous) (Skill 1.4)

   A.   The

   B.   fox

   C.   lazy

   D.   jumped

Answer: D. jumped
The suffix "-ed" is an affix that cannot stand alone as a unit of meaning. Thus it is bound to the free morpheme "jump." "The" is always an unbound morpheme since no suffix or prefix can alter its meaning. As written, "fox" and "lazy" are unbound, but their meaning is changed with affixes, such as "foxes" or "laziness."

7.   **Which of the following reading strategies calls for higher order cognitive skills?**
(Average) (Skill 1.5)

    A.   Making predictions

    B.   Summarizing

    C.   Monitoring

    D.   Making inferences

Answer: D: Making inferences
Making inferences from a reading text involves using other reading skills such as making predictions, skimming, scanning, summarizing, then coming to conclusions or making inferences which are not directly stated in the text.

8.   **Answering questions, monitoring comprehension, and interacting with a text are common methods of:**
(Average) (Skill 1.5)

    A.   Whole-class instruction

    B.   Comprehension instruction

    C.   Research-based instruction

    D.   Evidence-based instruction

Answer: B. Comprehension instruction
Comprehension instruction helps students learn strategies that they can use independently with any text. Answering questions, monitoring comprehension, and interacting with a text are a few strategies that teachers can teach to their students to help increase their comprehension. Research-based, evidence-based, and whole-class instruction relate to specific reading programs available.

9. **Mrs. Young is a first grade teacher trying to select a books that are "just right" for her students to read independently. She needs to consider which of the following:**
   (Rigorous) (Skill 1.5)

   A. Illustrations should support the meaning of the text.

   B. Content that relates to student interest and experiences

   C. Predictable text structures and language patterns

   D. All of the above

Answer: D. All of the above
It is important that all of the above factors be considered when selecting books for young children.

10. **Which of the following is NOT a characteristic of a fable?**
    (Easy) (Skill 1.6)

    A. Animals that feel and talk like humans

    B. Happy solutions to human dilemmas

    C. Teaches a moral or standard for behavior

    D. Illustrates specific people or groups without directly naming them

Answer: D. Illustrates specific people or groups without directly naming them
A fable is a short tale with animals, humans, gods, or even inanimate objects as characters. Fables often conclude with a moral, delivered in the form of an epigram (a short, witty, and ingenious statement in verse). Fables are among the oldest forms of writing in human history: it appears in Egyptian papyri of c. 1500 BC. The most famous fables are those of Aesop, a Greek slave living in about 600 BC. In India, the Pantchatantra appeared in the third century. The most famous modern fables are those of seventeenth-century French poet Jean de La Fontaine.

11. **The children's literature genre came into its own in the:**
    (Average) (Skill 1.6)

    A.   Seventeenth century

    B.   Eighteenth century

    C.   Nineteenth century

    D.   Twentieth century

Answer: B. Eighteenth century
In the eighteenth century, authors such as Jean de La Fontaine and his Fables, Pierre Perrault's Tales, Mme. d'Aulnoye's novels based on old folktales, and Mme. de Beaumont's Beauty and the Beast all created a children's literature genre. In England, Perrault was translated and a work allegedly written by Oliver Smith, The Renowned History of Little Goody Two Shoes, also helped to establish children's literature in England.

12. **Which of the following is NOT characteristic of a folktale?**
    (Average) (Skill 1.6)

    A.   Considered true among various societies

    B.   A hero on a quest

    C.   Good versus evil

    D.   Adventures of animals

Answer: A. Considered true among various societies
There are few societies that would consider folktales to be true as folktale is another name for fairy tale, and elements such as heroes on a quest, good versus evil, and adventures of animals are popular, fictional, themes in fairy tales.

13. In her kindergarten class, Mrs. Thomas has been watching the students in the drama center. She has watched the children pretend to complete a variety of magic tricks. Mrs. Thomas decides to use stories about magic to share with her class. Her decision to incorporate their interests into the reading shows that Mrs. Thomas understands that:
(Average) (Skill 1.6)

   A.   Including student interests is important at all times

   B.   Teaching by themes is crucial for young children

   C.   Young children respond to literature that reflects their lives

   D.   Science fiction and fantasy are the most popular genres

Answer: C. Young children respond to literature that reflects their lives
Children's literature is intended to instruct students through entertaining stories, while also promoting an interest in the very act of reading, itself. Young readers respond best to themes that reflect their lives.

14. Which is an untrue statement about a theme in literature?
(Rigorous) (Skill 1.7)

   A.   The theme is always stated directly somewhere in the text

   B.   The theme is the central idea in a literary work

   C.   All parts of the work (plot, setting, mood should contribute to the theme in some way

   D.   By analyzing the various elements of the work, the reader should be able to arrive at an indirectly stated theme

Answer: A. The theme is always stated directly somewhere in the text
The theme may be stated directly, but it can also be implicit in various aspects of the work, such as the interaction between characters, symbolism, or description.

15. **Which of the following is an opinion?**
    (Easy) (Skill 1.7)

    A.   The sky is blue

    B.   Albany is the capital of New York State

    C.   A dog is the best pet to have

    D.   Humans breathe

Answer: C. A dog is the best pet to have
An opinion is a subjective evaluation based upon personal bias.

16. **Which is NOT a true statement concerning an author's literary tone?**
    (Rigorous) (Skill 1.7)

    A.   Tone is partly revealed through the selection of details

    B.   Tone is the expression of the author's attitude toward his/her subject

    C.   Tone in literature is usually satiric or angry

    D.   Tone in literature corresponds to the tone of voice a speaker uses

Answer: C. Tone in literature is usually satiric or angry
Tone in literature conveys a mood and can be as varied as the tone of voice of a speaker (see choice D., e.g. sad, nostalgic, whimsical, angry, formal, intimate, satirical, sentimental, etc.).

17. **Which of the following is an example of nonfiction literature?**
    (Average) (Skill 1.7)

    A.   Letters

    B.   Biographies

    C.   Journals

    D.   All of the above

Answer: D. All of the above
All of these are examples of nonfiction literature. Fiction is a made-up story; nonfiction relies on facts and data.

18. **A student has written a paper with the following characteristics: written in first person; characters, setting, and plot; some dialogue; events organized in chronological sequence with some flashbacks. In what genre has the student written?**
    (Easy) (Skill 1.7)

    A.   Expository writing

    B.   Narrative writing

    C.   Persuasive writing

    D.   Technical writing

Answer: B. Narrative writing
These are all characteristics of narrative writing. Expository writing is intended to give information, such as an explanation or directions, and the information is logically organized. Persuasive writing gives an opinion in an attempt to convince the reader that this point of view is valid or tries to persuade the reader to take a specific action. The goal of technical writing is to clearly communicate a select piece of information to a targeted reader or group of readers for a particular purpose in such a way that the subject can readily be understood. It is persuasive writing that anticipates a response from the reader.

19. **Which of the following is important in understanding fiction?**
(Rigorous) (Skill 1.7)

I.   Realizing the artistry in telling a story to convey a point.
II.   Knowing fiction is imaginary.
III.   Seeing what is truth and what is perspective.
IV.   Acknowledging the difference between opinion and truth.

A.   I and II only

B.   II and IV only

C.   III and IV only

D.   IV only

Answer: A. I and II only
In order to understand a piece of fiction, it is important that readers realize that an author's choice in a work of fiction is for the sole purpose of conveying a viewpoint. It is also important to understand that fiction is imaginary. Seeing what is truth and what is perspective and acknowledging the difference between opinion and truth are important in understanding nonfiction.

20. **All of the following are correctly capitalized EXCEPT:**
(Average) (Skill 1.8)

A.   Queen Elizabeth

B.   Congressman McKay

C.   Commander Alger

D.   The President of the United States

Answer: C. Commander Alger
If the statement read "Alger the commander" then commander would not need to be capitalized; however, because commander is the title it is capitalized.

21. **All of the following are correctly punctuated EXCEPT:**
    (Rigorous) (Skill 1.8)

    A.   "The book is on the table," said Bill's mother.

    B.   "Who would like to sing 'The Star Spangled Banner'?" the teacher asked.

    C.   I was embarrassed when Joanne said, "The meeting started an hour ago!"

    D.   "The policeman apprehended the criminals last night."

Answer: C: I was embarrassed when Joanne said, "The meeting started an hour ago!"
In sentences that are interrogatory or exclamatory, the question mark or exclamation point should be positioned outside the closing quotation marks if the quote itself is a statement or command or cited title. The sentence should read:
I was embarrassed when Joanne said, "The meeting started an hour ago"!

22. **Which of the following sentences contains a subject-verb agreement error?**
    (Average) (Skill 1.8)

    A.   Both mother and her two sisters were married in a triple ceremony.

    B.   Neither the hen nor the rooster is likely to be served for dinner.

    C.   My boss, as well as the company's two personnel directors, have been to Spain.

    D.   Amanda and the twins are late again.

Answer: C. My boss, as well as the company's two personnel directors, have been to Spain.
In choice C, the true subject of the verb is "My boss," not "two personnel directors." Because the subject is singular, the verb form must be singular, "has." In choices A and D, the compound subjects are joined by "and" and take the plural form of the verb. In choice B, the compound subject is joined by "nor" so the verb must agree with the subject closer to the verb. "Rooster" is singular so the correct verb is "is."

23. **Which of the following are punctuated correctly?**
    (Rigorous) (Skill 1.8)

    I.   The teacher directed us to compare Faulkner's three symbolic
            novels Absalom, Absalom; As I Lay Dying; and Light in August.
    II.   Three of Faulkner's symbolic novels are: Absalom, Absalom; As I
            Lay Dying; and Light in August.
    III.   The teacher directed us to compare Faulkner's three symbolic
            novels: Absalom, Absalom; As I Lay Dying; and Light in August.
    IV.   Three of Faulkner's symbolic novels are Absalom, Absalom; As I Lay
            Dying; and Light in August.

    A.   I and II only

    B.   II and III only

    C.   III and IV only

    D.   IV only

Answer: C. III and IV only
These sentences are focusing on the use of a colon. The rule is to place a colon at the
beginning of a list of items except when the list is preceded by a verb. Sentences I and
III do not have a verb before the list and therefore need a colon. Sentences II and IV
have a verb before the list, and therefore do not need a colon.

24. **If a student uses inappropriate language that includes slang and expletives, what is the best course of action to take in order to influence the student's formal communication skills?**
(Rigorous) (Skill 1.10)

    A.   Ask the student to paraphrase the writing, that is, translate it into language appropriate for the school principal to read

    B.   Refuse to read the student's papers until he conforms to a more literate style

    C.   Ask the student to read his work aloud to the class for peer evaluation

    D.   Rewrite the flagrant passages to show the student the right form of expression

Answer: A. Ask the student to paraphrase the writing, that is, translate it into language appropriate for the school principal to read
Asking the student to write for a specific audience will help him become more involved in his writing. If he continues writing to the same audience—the teacher—he will continue seeing writing as just another assignment, and he will not apply grammar, vocabulary, and syntax the way they should be. By paraphrasing his own writing, the student will learn to write for a different public.

25. **Which of the following is an example of alliteration?**
(Average) (Skill 2.1)

    A.   "The City's voice itself is soft like Solitude."

    B.   "Both in one faith unanimous; though sad"

    C.   "By all their country's wishes blest!"

    D.   "In earliest Greece to these with partial choice."

Answer: A: "The City's voice itself is soft like Solitude."
Alliteration is the repetition of consonant sounds in two or more neighboring words or syllables, usually the beginning sound but not always. This line from Shelley's Stanzas Written in Dejection Near Naples is an especially effective use of alliteration using the sibilant s not only at the beginning of words but also within words. Alliteration usually appears in prosody; however, effective use of alliteration can be found in other genres.

26. **According to Marilyn Jager Adams, which skill would a student demonstrate by identifying that cat does not belong in the group of words containing dog, deer, and dress?**
(Average) (Skill 2.1)

A. Recognize the odd member in a group

B. Replace sounds in words

C. Count the sounds in a word

D. Count syllables in a word

Answer: A. Recognize the odd member in a group
One of Marilyn Jager Adams' basic types of phonemic awareness tasks involves the ability to do oddity tasks, which involves recognizing the member of a set that is different among the group. In this example, the word cat is the odd member because it starts with a different sound.

27. **Which of the following is NOT a characteristic of a good reader?**
(Rigorous) (Skill 2.4)

A. When faced with unfamiliar words, they skip over them unless meaning is lost

B. They formulate questions that they predict will be answered in the text

C. They establish a purpose before reading

D. They go back to reread when something doesn't make sense

Answer: A. When faced with unfamiliar words, they skip over them unless meaning is lost.
While skipping over an unknown word may not compromise the meaning of the text, a good reader will attempt to pronounce the word by using analogies to familiar words. They also formulate questions, establish a purpose, and go back to reread if meaning is lost.

28. **Which of the following is NOT a strategy of teaching reading comprehension?**
   (Rigorous) (Skill 2.5)

   A.   Summarization

   B.   Utilizing graphic organizers

   C.   Manipulating sounds

   D.   Having students generate questions

Answer: C. Manipulating sounds
Comprehension simply means that the reader can ascribe meaning to text. Teachers can use many strategies to teach comprehension, including questioning, asking students to paraphrase or summarize, utilizing graphic organizers, and focusing on mental images.

29. **Which of the following is NOT a technique of prewriting?**
   (Average) (Skill 2.6)

   A.   Clustering

   B.   Listing

   C.   Brainstorming

   D.   Proofreading

Answer: D. Proofreading
Proofreading cannot be a method of prewriting, since it is done on already written texts only.

30. **Which of the following is NOT an approach to keep students ever conscious of the need to write for audience appeal?**
(Rigorous) (Skill 2.6)

   A.   Pairing students during the writing process

   B.   Reading all rough drafts before the students write the final copies

   C.   Having students compose stories or articles for publication in school literary magazines or newspapers

   D.   Writing letters to friends or relatives

Answer: D. Writing letters to friends or relatives
Reading all rough drafts will not encourage the students to take control of their text and might even inhibit their creativity. On the contrary, pairing students will foster their sense of responsibility, and having them compose stories for literary magazines will boost their self-esteem as well as their organization skills. As far as writing letters is concerned, the work of authors such as Madame de Sevigne in the seventeenth century is a good example of epistolary literary work.

31. **Which of the following mostly addresses grammatical and technical errors?**
(Easy) (Skill 2.6)

   A.   Revising

   B.   Editing

   C.   Proofreading

   D.   Rough draft writing

Answer: C. Proofreading
During the proofreading process grammatical and technical errors are addressed. The other choices indicate times when writing or rewriting is taking place.

32. **All of the following are stages of the writing process EXCEPT:**
   (Average) (Skill 2.6)

   A.   Prewriting

   B.   Revising

   C.   Organizing

   D.   Presenting

Answer: D. Presenting
Writing is a process that can be clearly defined. First, students must prewrite to discover ideas, materials, experiences, sources, etc. Next, they must organize and determine their purpose, thesis, and supporting details. Last, they must edit and revise to polish the paper. While presenting is a nice finale to the writing process, it is not necessary for a complete and polished work.

33. **Which of the following is true about semantics?**
   (Average) (Skill 2.7)

   A.   Semantics will sharpen the effect and meaning of a text

   B.   Semantics refers to the meaning expressed when words are arranged in a specific way

   C.   Semantics is a vocabulary instruction technique

   D.   Semantics is representing spoken language through the use of symbols

Answer: B. Semantics refers to the meaning expressed when words are arranged in a specific way
Understanding semantics means understanding that meaning is imbedded in the order of words in a sentence. Changing the order of the words would change the meaning of a sentence. The other three choices do not involve finding meaning through the order of words.

34. **Jose moved to the United States last month. He speaks little or no English at this time. His teacher is teaching the class about habitats in science and has chosen to read a story about various habitats to the class. The vocabulary is difficult. What should Jose's teacher do with Jose?**
(Rigorous) (Skill 2.7)

   A.   Provide Jose with additional opportunities to learn about habitats

   B.   Read the story to Jose multiple times

   C.   Show Jose pictures of habitats from his native country

   D.   Excuse Jose from the assignment

Answer A. Provide Jose with additional opportunities to learn about habitats
Students who are learning English should be exposed to a variety of opportunities to learn the same concepts as native speakers. Content should not be changed, but the manner in which it is presented and reinforced should be changed.

35. **John is having difficulty reading the word reach. In isolation, he pronounces each sound as /r/ /ee/ /sh/. Which of the following is a possible instructional technique which could help solve John's reading difficulty?**
(Rigorous) (Skill 3.1)

   A.   Additional phonemic awareness instruction

   B.   Additional phonics instruction

   C.   Additional skill and drill practice

   D.   Additional minimal pair practice

Answer: A. Additional phonemic awareness instruction
John is having difficulty with the sound symbol relationship between the /ch/ and /sh/. While it may appear at first that this is a phonics problem, in fact, it is important to begin with the earlier skill of phonemic awareness to ensure the student has a solid foundational understanding of the oral portions before moving totally into the sound symbol arena. If John is able to distinguish between the two sounds orally, it is obvious more phonics instruction is needed. However, proceeding directly to phonics instruction may be pointless and frustrating for John if he is unable to hear the distinctions.

36. **To decode is to:**
    (Easy) (Skill 3.2)

      A.   Construct meaning

      B.   Sound out a printed sequence of letters

      C.   Use a special code to decipher a message

      D.   None of the above

Answer: B. Sound out a printed sequence of letters
To decode means to change communication signals into messages. Reading comprehension requires that the reader learn the code within which a message is written and be able to decode it to get the message.

37. **Which of the following is a formal reading level assessment?**
    (Easy) (Skill 3.2)

      A.   A standardized reading test

      B.   A teacher-made reading test

      C.   An interview

      D.   A reading diary

Answer: A. A standardized reading test
If an assessment is standardized, it has to be objective, whereas choices B, C, and D are all subjective assessments.

38. **Which of the following is NOT one of the metalinguistic abilities acquired by children from early involvement in reading activities?**
(Rigorous) (Skill 3.3)

   A.   Conventions of print

   B.   Word consciousness

   C.   Spelling fluency

   D.   Functions of print

Answer: C. Spelling fluency
Conventions of print, word consciousness, and functions of print are all learned from children's early involvement with reading. Spelling fluency is learned a little later on in reading and a fluent speller is often good at reading comprehension.

39. **The English department is developing strategies to encourage all students to become a community of readers. From the list of suggestions below, which would be the least effective way for teachers to foster independent reading?**
(Average) (Skill 3.3)

   A.   Each teacher will set aside a weekly 30-minute in-class reading session during which the teacher and students read a magazine or book for enjoyment

   B.   Teacher and students develop a list of favorite books to share with each other

   C.   The teacher assigns at least one book report each grading period to ensure that students are reading from the established class list

   D.   The students gather books for a classroom library so that books may be shared with each other

Answer: C. The teacher assigns at least one book report each grading period to ensure that students are reading from the established class list
Teacher-directed assignments, such as book reports, appear routine and unexciting. Students will be more excited about reading when they can actively participate. In choice A, the teacher is modeling reading behavior and providing students with a dedicated time during which time they can read independently and still be surrounded by a community of readers. In choices B and D, students share and make available their reading choices.

40. **As Ms. Wolmark looks at the mandated vocabulary curriculum for the 5th grade, she notes that she can opt to teach foreign words and abbreviations which have become part of the English language. She decides:**
(Rigorous) (Skill 3.3)

   A.   To forego that since she is not a teacher of foreign language.

   B.   To teach only foreign words from the native language of her four ELL students.

   C.   To use the ELL students' native languages as a start for an extensive study of foreign language words.

   D.   To teach 2-3 foreign language words that are now in English and let it go at that.

Answer: C. To use the ELL students' native languages as a start for an extensive study of foreign language words.
Incorporating the native language of ELL students into instruction helps to form a bond between their native language and English. It also serves as a point of confidence that connects that student with the other students in the class.

41. **Which of the following is a convention of print that children learn during reading activities?**
(Average) (Skill 3.3)

   A.   The meaning of words

   B.   The left to right motion

   C.   The purpose of print

   D.   The identification of letters

Answer B: The left to right motion
During reading activities, children learn conventions of print. Children learn the way to hold a book, where to begin to read, the left to right motion, and how to continue from one line to another.

42. Reading a piece of student writing to assess the overall impression of the product is
(Average) (Skill 3.7)

    A.   Holistic evaluation

    B.   Portfolio assessment

    C.   Analytical evaluation

    D.   Using a performance system

Answer: A. Holistic evaluation
Holistic scoring assesses a piece of writing as a whole. Usually a paper is read quickly through once to get a general impression. The writing is graded according to the impression of the whole work rather than the sum of its parts. Often holistic scoring uses a rubric that establishes the overall criteria for a certain score to evaluate each paper.

Answer Key: Reading

1.	A	22.	C
2.	D	23.	C
3.	A	24.	A
4.	D	25.	A
5.	B	26.	A
6.	D	27.	A
7.	D	28.	C
8.	B	29.	D
9.	D	30.	D
10.	D	31.	C
11.	B	32.	D
12.	A	33.	B
13.	C	34.	A
14.	A	35.	A
15.	C	36.	B
16.	C	37.	A
17.	D	38.	C
18.	B	39.	C
19.	A	40.	C
20.	C	41.	B
21.	C	42.	A

Rigor Table: Reading

	Easy 14.3%	Average 45.2%	Rigorous 40.5%
Questions	10, 15, 18, 31, 36, 37	1, 2, 3, 7, 8, 11, 12, 13, 17, 20, 22, 25, 26, 29, 32, 33, 39, 41, 42	4, 5, 6, 9, 14, 16, 19, 21, 23, 24, 27, 28, 30, 34, 35, 38, 40

READING ESSAYS

Sean is five years old and in kindergarten. He is precocious and seems to have a lot of energy throughout the day. Sean has a hard time settling down in the classroom, and the teacher often needs to redirect him in order to have him complete assignments. Sean is struggling in many areas, but currently his lowest area is in writing. Though it is January, Sean still does not seem to be making the appropriate sound symbol connection to make progress with his writing. Sean still needs to be reminded to use a tripod grasp on his pencil and often slips into a fist grip. His drawings are rushed and lack detail but are recognizable. Sean has made some progress with his skills though. At the beginning of the year, he was unable to make any recognizable letters. Now he always makes letters when he is writing; however, there are rarely spaces between the letters. Sean's progress in this area is significantly behind his peers, and you have decided to design an intervention plan to address these concerns.

How would you prioritize the areas where Sean is struggling within your intervention plan and provide justification as to why you would prioritize them in this manner? What instructional activities would you implement as part of the intervention plan? Finally, where else could you seek support and ideas for things to help address Sean's writing skills?

Sample Good Response

The first step in creating any intervention plan for a student is to prioritize the areas in which the student is struggling. In Sean's case, there are many different areas where he is struggling. The first one I would address is the sound symbol connection. I would choose this area because in order for any student to be able to complete any type of writing assignment, they need to have an understanding of what sounds letters make. If Sean does not know that the letter b makes the /b/ sound, then when he is sounding out words and comes across the /b/ sound, he will have no idea what symbol to write for that sound. In order to address this skill, I would incorporate a great deal of phonemic awareness activities to develop Sean's sound symbol awareness. If I was unable to make progress or lacking in appropriate activities, I could seek support from a colleague or a reading specialist to obtain further ideas.

After this, I would work on spacing. In this area, I would use a tool that Sean could use to help him create spaces in his writing. A clothespin works well and can be given a face with a marker to be called a spaceman. The spaceman can be used by Sean to lie down on his paper after every word he writes so that he has an appropriate sized space between words. Eventually, this tool can be weaned away from Sean as he learns to create appropriate spaces without the tool.

Finally, I would address Sean's lack of the use of a tripod grasp by providing him with broken crayons to use multiple times throughout the day. When children use small pieces of crayons, the hands automatically form the appropriate grasp in order to hold such a small writing tool. When he has to write, there are special pencil grips or pencils that encourage the appropriate grasp as well. I would consult with the schools occupational therapist assigned to my school for further ideas and suggestions to improve Sean's fine motor schools.

Sample Poor Response

I would start with talking to Sean's parents about his inability to focus. If Sean could pay better attention, he would be able to write more appropriately. Having a parent teacher conference would help the parents to see how Sean is struggling within the classroom and seek out help from doctors to address his attention issues.

Then I would work on spelling activities with him. By giving Sean words to learn and memorize, he will be able to transfer these to his writing. If he was able to already know how to spell words, he will be more able to write things correctly. This will help him to be able to write more like his peers.

Finally, I would give him sentences with one blank to fill in, rather than letting him come up with his own ideas. If he only has to focus on one idea, he will be more likely to be able to be successful than having to think of the entire sentence.

MATHEMATICS

1. **Preschool children are learning to count by teaching them a song. What method are you using?**
    (Easy) (Skill 4.1)

    A.   Rote counting

    B.   Guessing

    C.   Memory

    D.   Cite counting

Answer: A. Rote counting
A good way to tech preschool children to count is to use rote counting, where they repeat the numbers over and over in sequence or in order.

2. **You are teaching a lesson on converting a decimal to a percent. How do you explain to students how to change a decimal to a percent?**
    (Average) (Skill 4.1)

    A.   Divide by 100 or move the decimal point 2 places to the left

    B.   Write the decimal as a fraction and then divided the numerator by the denominator

    C.   Multiply the decimal by 100 or move the decimal point 2 places to the right

    D.   Add a percent symbol

Answer: C. Multiply the decimal by 100 or move the decimal point 2 places to the right
To covert a decimal to a percent, you multiply by 100 or you can just move the decimal point 2 places to the right.

3. **The mathematical statement illustrates what property.**
   (Rigorous) (Skill 4.1)

   a • 1 = a

   A.   Inverse property of multiplication

   B.   Identity property of multiplication

   C.   Commutative property of multiplication

   D.   Associative property of multiplication

Answer: B. Identity property of multiplication
The number 1 is the multiplicative identity. Any non-zero number multiplied by 1 is that number.

4. **Which operation is used to solve the following application problem:**
   (Average) (Skill 4.1)

   You are hosting a surprise anniversary party. You plan to invite 145 people. The cost of mailing a letter or card $0.44. How much will it cost to send the invitations?

   A.   Addition

   B.   Subtraction

   C.   Division

   D.   Multiplication

Answer: D. Multiplication
You use multiplication because you want to find the total cost. The total cost is the number if invitations by the cost to mail each invitation.

5. You give your pre-school students this problem. What level of mathematics are you beginning to teach your students?
    (Average) (Skill 4.2)

    State the missing figure in the pattern.

    A.   Geometry

    B.   Pre-algebra and Algebra

    C.   Trigonometry

    D.   Basic Math

Answer: B. Pre-algebra and Algebra
In primary grades, pre-algebra and algebra is developed through learning about patterns.

6. **Name the triangle.**
    (Easy) (Skill 4.3)

    A.   Right triangle

    B.   Acute triangle

    C.   Equilateral triangle

    D.   Isosceles triangle

Answer: D. isosceles triangle
The triangle is an isosceles triangle because toe sides of the triangle are the same length.

7. **What characteristic classifies a polygon as regular?**
   (Rigorous) (Skill 4.3)

   A.   All sides have the same length and all angles have the same measure

   B.   All angles have the same measure

   C.   All sides are of different length, and all angle measures are different

   D.   All sides are the same length

Answer: A. All sides have the same length, and all angles have the same measure
In a regular polygon all sides have the same length and all angles have the same measure.

8. **The following definition describes what type of figure. Give an example of the figure.**
   (Rigorous) (Skill 4.3)

   The union of all points on a simple closed surface and all points in its interior forms a space figure.

   A.   solid; rectangle

   B.   solid; sphere

   C.   polyhedra; cone

   D.   polygon; sphere

Answer: B solid; sphere
The definition describes a solid. An example of a solid is a sphere.

9. **The following tessellation uses what type of transformational symmetry?**
   (Average) (Skill 4.3)

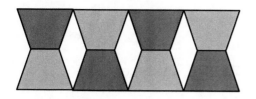

   A.   Rotation

   B.   Translation

   C.   Glide reflection

   D.   Rotation and translation

Answer: D. rotation and translation
The figure shows a rotation and a translation. The original image is translated to the right and then rotated 180°.

10. **Measures in pound and kilograms describe what type of measurement?**
    (Easy) (Skill 4.3)

    A.   Temperature

    B.   Weight

    C.   Liquid volume

    D.   Distance and area

Answer: B. Weight
Pounds and kilograms are units to measure weights.

11. **Find the mean, standard deviation, and variance of the test scores. Use a calculator.**
    (Average) (Skill 4.4)

    90, 75, 60, 90, 85

    A. Mean: 80, standard deviation: 12.74754878, variance: 162.5

    B. Mean: 12.74754878, standard deviation: 80, variance: 162.5

    C. Mean: 80, standard deviation: 162.5, variance: 12.74754878

    D. Mean: 90, standard deviation: 162.5 variance: 80

Answer: A. Mean: 80, standard deviation: 12.74754878, variance: 162.5
Use the calculator's mean, standard deviation, and variance functions to find the answers.

12. **You are teaching a class of first graders how to add and subtract. Which of the follow manipulatives are not useful in teaching these skills?**
    (Average) (Skill 5.1)

    A. Number lines

    B. Algebra tiles

    C. Counters

    D. Jelly beans, raisins, chocolate chips, etc

Answer: B. Algebra tiles
Algebra tiles are not helpful at this level.

13. **You would like to teach your students that math is important in their lives. Which activity listed below would not be a good activity for your student to do to show them math in their everyday lives?**
(Rigorous) (Skill 5.1)

A.   Research a mathematician

B.   Design a playground

C.   Bake a batch of cookies and measure the ingredients

D.   Chart the weather on a daily basis

Answer: A. Research a mathematician
While learning about a mathematician can be a good learning experience, it does not teach students about math in their daily lives.

14. **Your students were assigned a cross-curricular activity, math and social studies One of your students compared the rainfall amounts, for one year, of the United States and China. What type of display would not display the data in a meaningful way?**
(Rigorous) (Skill 5.1)

A.   Line graph

B.   Bar chart

C.   Circle graph

D.   Table

Answer: C. Circle graph
A circle graph is best used to show the amount of data as a slice of a circle, usually measured in percent.

15. **You are introducing a unit on measurement to your second graders. You want to start with a fun activity to engage your students. Which of the following activities could you use?**
    (Average) (Skill 5.1)

    A.   Talk about distance using a map

    B.   Begin by discussing the Customary and Metric measurement systems

    C.   Talk about distance by using a replica of the solar system

    D.   Have students bring in a shoe from home; ask them to measure the distance from wall-to-wall using the shoe; then discuss the different amount of shoe lengths student get.

Answer: D. Have students bring in a shoe from home; ask them to measure the distance from wall-to-wall using the shoe; then discuss the different amount of shoe lengths student get
This activity will get students to understand the "foot" measurement. It will also introduce them to the idea of a "standard" in measurement,

16. **Problem solving spans across the curriculum. In math, problem solving is usually presented in the form of "word problems" or real world applications. What is the first step you teach your students in problem solving?**
    (Easy) (Skill 5.2)

    A.   Understand the problem

    B.   Devise a plan

    C.   Carry out the plan

    D.   Look back

Answer: A. Understand the problem
The key to problem solving is to make sure you understand the problem. Understanding the words, pictures, diagrams; knowing if there is enough information to solve the problem; and knowing what you are asked to do.

17. **How would you teach your students to solve this problem?**
    (Average) (Skill 5.2)

    The scale on a map is 1 inch = 50 miles. How many miles are there in 7 inches?

    A.   Pick a point on a map and draw a circle with a diameter of 7 inches

    B.   Use a map with the same scale and measure 7 inches.

    C.   Use a proportion

    D.   Use estimation

Answer: C. Use a proportion
Proportions can be used to solve problems where relationships are compared.
$\dfrac{1}{50} = \dfrac{7}{x}$ after cross multiplication

$x = 7 \times 50$

$x = 350.$

7 inches on the map is equal to 350 miles.

18. **You are teaching your students to solve problems involving percents. When working with percents, what must you tell your students to do to the percent before it can be used in solving a problem?**
    (Easy) (Skill 5.2)

    A.   Change the percent to a whole number

    B.   Do not change anything

    C.   Drop the percent symbol

    D.   Change the percent to a decimal

Answer: D. Change the percent to a decimal
Percent means out of 100. Before a percent can be used in any operation, it must be changed to a decimal by moving the decimal point 2 places to the left.

19. **Why are manipulatives useful in teaching mathematics?**
    (Rigorous) (Skill 5.3)

    A. Manipulatives make math fun

    B. Allow students to understand mathematical concepts by allowing them to see concrete examples of abstract processes

    C. Give the teacher a change of pace with instruction

    D. Students like playing with them

Answer: B. Allow students to understand mathematical concepts by allowing them to see concrete examples of abstract processes
Some students have trouble visualizing mathematical concepts. If the concept can be shown using a manipulative, the student can make the connection between abstract and concrete.

20. **Technology is becoming helpful in teaching math. Which answer does not explain why?**
    (Rigorous) (Skill 5.3)

    A. Students have been using technology and playing video games before they were enrolled in school making them very adept at using computers

    B. Technology can be used to give individualized help to each student

    C. Using technology gives the teacher a break from teaching

    D. With technology programs, students can learn at their own pace and gain confidence in their ability to do math.

Answer: C. Using technology gives the teacher a break from teaching
Technology is not a replacement for the teacher. It is to be used to complement one's teaching.

21. **Why is planning some formal assessment during a lesson important?**
(Average) (Skill 6.1)

   A.   It gives the teacher a break from teaching

   B.   It allows students a chance to catch up on the material if they are behind

   C.   It allows the teacher to make sure all students understand the material. If they are not, it allows the teacher an opportunity to adjust the instruction

   D.   It's not a good idea to use formal assessment during a lesson

Answer: C It allows the teacher to make sure all students understand the material. If they are not, it allows the teacher an opportunity to adjust the instruction
Teachers need a way to make sure students understand the material. One or two questions asked at different parts of the lesson will let the teacher know if students understand the material.

22. **Observation is the most effective method used when problem solving. Which answer is not an example of an activity in which a teacher can observe students to be sure they are understanding the material.**
(Rigorous) (Skill 6.2)

   A.   Watch students taking a test

   B.   Plan a cooperative activity for you students

   C.   Plan a game for the students that involves the math concepts you are teaching

   D.   Divide the class into groups, give each group a problem to solve where each student of the group must do a part of the problem

Answer: A. Watch students taking a test
Watching students taking a test does not help you assess whether or not students understand the material. It's only after you correct the test that you can gauge students understanding of the math.

Answer Key: Mathematics

1. A	12. B
2. C	13. A
3. B	14. C
4. D	15. D
5. B	16. A
6. D	17. C
7. A	18. D
8. B	19. B
9. D	20. C
10. B	21. C
11. A	22. A

Rigor Table: Mathematics

	Easy 22.7%	Average 40.9%	Rigorous 36.3%
Questions	1, 6, 10, 16, 18	2, 4, 5, 9, 11, 12, 15, 17, 21	3, 7, 8, 13, 14, 19, 20, 22

Math Essays

You have designed an alternative assessment based on a portfolio, observation, and oral presentation for a student with learning disabilities in the area of reading and writing. Your colleague is concerned that this lowers expectations for the student, deprives him of the chance to practice taking the kind of tests he needs to be successful and sets him further apart from the other students.

Justify your choice of an alternative assessment for the learning-disabled student in place of the traditional tests that other students are taking. How would you respond to your colleague's concerns and reassure her that the assessment you are planning is valid and in the best interests of the student?

Sample Response

The primary purpose of assessment is to support the academic growth of a child. Thus, assessment must provide an accurate picture of the skills and knowledge that a child has acquired. This goal overrides all other considerations, however valid they might be. The student who has difficulty with reading and writing will be at a disadvantage in a written and timed test. Thus, having him take the standard test with everyone will provide erroneous feedback about his real skills and understanding of content. The alternative assessment plan, on the other hand, gives the learning-disabled student an opportunity to show what he knows and gives the teacher more detailed and accurate feedback that can be used to modify and enhance the curriculum and teaching methods used for him. The portfolio and observation will allow the teacher to evaluate him based on multiple pieces of information gathered over a period of time. The oral presentation will allow him to express his knowledge using his strengths rather than his weaknesses. This will not only help him feel more confident and successful, it will help the teacher to better address his needs so that he can overcome his reading and writing difficulties in the long run.

My colleague's concerns are valid and must be kept in mind while planning a long-term approach to educating the learning-disabled student. While alternative assessments are called for in the short term, as the student progresses, he must be trained and supported so that he is eventually able to take standard tests with other students. Care must be taken not to lower expectations in the alternative assessment. Clearly defined rubrics supporting high standards for the portfolio and oral presentation will ensure that this does not happen. The rubrics will be clearly explained to the student in advance.

Finally, the goal of alternative assessment is to help the student's eventual integration with the rest of the class. It is his disability that currently sets him apart. A well-planned assessment structure feeding into enhanced instructional support will help close the gap.

SCIENCE

1. **What does a primary consumer most commonly refer to?**
   (Average) (Skill 7.1)

   A. Herbivore

   B. Autotroph

   C. Carnivore

   D. Decomposer

Answer A: Herbivore
Autotrophs are the primary producers of the ecosystem. Producers mainly consist of plants. Primary consumers are the next trophic level. The primary consumers are the herbivores that eat plants or algae. Secondary consumers are the carnivores that eat the primary consumers. Tertiary consumers eat the secondary consumer. These trophic levels may go higher, depending on the ecosystem.

2. **All of the following are oceans EXCEPT:**
   (Easy) (Skill 7.2)

   A. Pacific

   B. Atlantic

   C. Mediterranean

   D. Indian

Answer: C. Mediterranean
The Mediterranean is a sea, which is smaller than an ocean and surrounded by land.

3. **What type of rock can be classified by the size of the crystals in the rock?**
    (Easy) (Skill 7.2)

    A.   Metamorphic

    B.   Igneous

    C.   Minerals

    D.   Sedimentary

Answer: B. Igneous
Igneous rock is formed when molten rock material cools. It is characterized by its grain size and mineral content. Metamorphic rocks are formed from other rocks as a result of heat and pressure. Sedimentary rocks come from weathering and erosion of pre existing rocks.

4. **What are solids with a definite chemical composition and a tendency to split along planes of weakness?**
    (Easy) (Skill 7.2)

    A.   Ores

    B.   Rocks

    C.   Minerals

    D.   Salts

Answer: C. Rocks
Rocks are made up of minerals, and ores are rocks than can be processed for a commercial use. Salts are ionic compounds formed from acids and bases.

5.   **What is a large, rotating, low-pressure system accompanied by heavy precipitation and strong winds known as?**
     (Easy) (Skill 7.2)

     A.   A hurricane

     B.   A tornado

     C.   A thunderstorm

     D.   A tsunami

Answer A. A hurricane
Hurricanes are storms that develop when warm, moist air carried by trade winds rotates around a low-pressure "eye." These form a large, rotating, low-pressure system and are accompanied by heavy precipitation and strong winds. They are also known as tropical cyclones or typhoons.

6.   **The breakdown of rock due to acid rain is an example of:**
     (Rigorous) (Skill 7.2)

     A.   Physical weathering

     B.   Frost wedging

     C.   Chemical weathering

     D.   Deposition

Answer: C. Chemical weathering
The breaking down of rocks at or near to the earth's surface is known as weathering. Chemical weathering is the breaking down of rocks through changes in their chemical composition. The breakdown of rock due to acid rain is an example of chemical weathering.

7.   **The most abundant gas in the atmosphere is:**
     (Rigorous) (Skill 7.2)

     A.   Oxygen

     B.   Nitrogen

     C.   Carbon dioxide

     D.   Methane

Answer: B   Nitrogen
Nitrogen accounts for 78.09 percent of the atmosphere, oxygen 20.95 percent, carbon dioxide 0.03 percent, and methane does not make up any of the atmosphere.

8.   **Which of the following is an example of a chemical change?**
     (Rigorous) (Skill 7.3)

     A.   Freezing food to preserve it

     B.   Using baking powder in biscuits

     C.   Melting glass to make a vase

     D.   Mixing concrete with water

Answer: B. Using baking powder in biscuits
A **physical change** is a change that does not produce a new substance. The freezing and melting of water is an example of physical change. A **chemical change** (or **chemical reaction**) changes the inherent properties of a substance. This includes things such as burning materials that turn into smoke or a seltzer tablet that fizzes into gas bubbles when submerged in water.

9.   The main source of glucose in the human diet is:
     (Average) (Skill 7.4)

        A.   Carbohydrates

        B.   Fat

        C.   Protein

        D.   Most forms of food

Answer: A. Carbohydrates
Carbohydrates are the main source of energy (glucose) in the human diet. The two types of carbohydrates are simple and complex. **Complex carbohydrates** have greater nutritional value because they take longer to digest, contain dietary fiber, and do not excessively elevate blood sugar levels. Common sources of carbohydrates are fruits, vegetables, grains, dairy products, and legumes.

10. **Which scientist is credited with launching the Scientific Revolution in the 16th century?**
     (Rigorous) (Skill 8.1)

        A.   Roger Bacon

        B.   Nicolaus Copernicus

        C.   Johannes Kepler

        D.   Isaac Newton

Answer: B. Nicolaus Copernicus
Roger Bacon (1224–1294) is considered one of the early advocates of the scientific method. In the fourteenth century, there was scientific progress in kinematics, but the Scientific Revolution began in the sixteenth century with the heliocentric theory of Nicolaus Copernicus. In 1605, Johannes Kepler discovered that planets orbit the sun in elliptical, not circular paths. In 1677, Isaac Newton derived Kepler's laws from the second law of motion.

11. **An experiment is performed to determine the effects of acid rain on plant life. Which of the following would be the variable?**
    (Average) (Skill 8.2)

    A.   The type of plant

    B.   The amount of light

    C.   The pH of the water

    D.   The amount of water

Answer: C. The pH of the water
The variable is the value that is manipulated during the experiment. In order to determine proper cause and effect, the plant type, light, and amount of water should be kept the same for various plants, and the pH of the water should change.

12. **What is the last step in the scientific method?**
    (Easy) (Skill 8.2)

    A.   Pose a question

    B.   Draw a conclusion

    C.   Conduct a test

    D.   Record data

Answer B: Draw a conclusion
The steps in the scientific method, in order, are pose a question, form a hypothesis, conduct a test, observe and record data, and draw a conclusion.

13. An experiment is performed to determine how the surface area of a liquid affects how long it takes for the liquid to evaporate. One hundred milliliters of water is put in containers with surface areas of 10 cm^2, 30 cm^2, 50 cm^2, 70 cm^2, and 90 cm^2. The time it took for each container to evaporate is recorded. Which of the following is a controlled variable?
(Rigorous) (Skill 8.2)

    A.   The time required for each evaporation

    B.   The area of the surfaces

    C.   The amount of water

    D.   The temperature of the water

Answer: C. The amount of water
The surface area is the independent variable and the time is the dependent variable. The temperature of the water should have been controlled in this experiment.

Answer Key: Science

1. A	8. B
2. C	9. A
3. B	10. B
4. C	11. C
5. A	12. B
6. C	13. C
7. B	

Rigor Table: Science

	Easy 38.5%	Average 23%	Rigorous 38.5%
Questions	2, 3, 4, 5, 12	1, 9, 11	6, 7, 8, 10, 13

SCIENCE ESSAYS

A mechanical wave is a disturbance in a medium in which energy is propagated, but not bulk matter. Waves can be transverse or longitudinal. A wave has frequency, amplitude, and wavelength. The speed of a wave is determined by the medium.

What would be the instructional objective, lesson motivation, and student activity in a lesson about waves?

Sample Response
The instructional objective is that students will learn that waves travel in a medium and have a speed, amplitude, and frequency. A motivation should give students an incentive or reason to be interested in the lesson. The lesson can be motivated by asking students what sound is. Also, you can demonstrate a mechanical wavy by sending a series of pulses down a Slinky or a long spring. Send a single longitudinal pulse down a Slinky by compressing it over a small distance and releasing the deformation. Ask students what is moving and why. Demonstrate a transverse pulse and ask students to describe the difference. Use a different medium, such as a rope, to show different media have different speeds. The speed of a wave travelling down a spring can be increased by giving the spring different tensions. Elicit from students why the speed of the wave changes. Set up standing waves in a spring by sending waves in opposite directions. Discuss with students whether or not a standing wave is a wave or a vibration.

SOCIAL SCIENCES

1. **Which of the following is not one of the three main concepts of human-environment interaction?**
   (Easy) (Skill 10.1)

   A.   Adapt

   B.   Modify

   C.   Depend

   D.   Expand

Answer: D. Expand
The theme of human-environmental interaction has three main concepts: humans adapt to the environment (wearing warm clothing in a cold climate, for instance,) humans modify the environment (planting trees to block a prevailing wind, for example), and humans depend on the environment (for food, water and raw materials.)

2. **The Southern Hemisphere contains all of the following?**
   (Average) (Skill 10.1)

   A.   Africa

   B.   Australia

   C.   South America

   D.   North America

Answer: B. Australia
The Southern Hemisphere, located between the South Pole and the Equator, contains all of Australia, a small part of Asia, about one-third of Africa, most of South America, and all of Antarctica.

3. **What is the largest ocean on the planet?**
   (Easy) (Skill 10.1)

   A.   Indian Ocean

   B.   Pacific Ocean

   C.   Atlantic Ocean

   D.   Arctic Ocean

Answer: B. Pacific Ocean
Oceans are the largest bodies of water on the planet. The four oceans of the earth are the Atlantic Ocean, one-half the size of the Pacific and separating North and South America from Africa and Europe; the Pacific Ocean, covering almost one-third of the entire surface of the earth and separating North and South America from Asia and Australia; the Indian Ocean, touching Africa, Asia, and Australia; and the ice-filled Arctic Ocean, extending from North America and Europe to the North Pole. The waters of the Atlantic, Pacific, and Indian Oceans also touch the shores of Antarctica.

4. **Which best describes social history?**
   (Rigorous) (Skill 10.2)

   A.   The study of ancient texts

   B.   The study of politics of the past

   C.   The study of societies of the past

   D.   The study of history from a global perspective

Answer: C. The study of societies of the past
Specialized fields of historical study include the following:

- Social history: the approach to the study of history that views a period of time through the eyes of everyday people and is focused on emerging trends.
- Archaeology: study of prehistoric and historic human cultures through the recovery, documentation and analysis of material remains and environmental data.
- Art History: the study of changes in social context through art.
- Big History: study of history on a large scale across long time frames (since the Big Bang and up to the future) through a multi-disciplinary approach.
- Chronology: science of localizing historical events in time.
- Cultural history: the study of culture in the past.
- Diplomatic history: the study of international relations in the past.
- Economic History: the study of economies in the past.
- Military History: the study of warfare and wars in history and what is sometimes considered to be a sub-branch of military history, Naval History.
- Paleography: study of ancient texts.
- Political history: the study of politics in the past.
- Psychohistory: study of the psychological motivations of historical events.
- Historiography of science: study of the structure and development of science.
- Social History: the study of societies in the past.
- World History: the study of history from a global perspective.

5. **Which of the following is a weakness of "periodization"?**
   (Average) (Skill 10.2)

   A.   It is arbitrary

   B.   Facilitates understanding

   C.   Identifies similarities

   D.   Categorizes knowledge

Answer: A. it is arbitrary
The practice of dividing history into a number of discrete periods or blocks of time is called "periodization." Because history is continuous, all systems of periodization are arbitrary to some extent. However, dividing time into segments facilitates understanding of changes that occur over time and helps identify similarities of events, knowledge, and experience within the defined period. Further, some divisions of time into these periods apply only under specific circumstances.

6. **Which of the following are US citizens guaranteed?**
   (Easy) (Skill 10.3)

   A.   Employment

   B.   Post-Secondary Education

   C.   Driver's License

   D.   Free Speech

Answer: D. Free Speech
In the United States, citizens are guaranteed the right to free speech: i.e., the right to express an opinion on public issues. In turn, citizens have the responsibility to allow others to speak freely. At the community level, this might mean speaking at a city council hearing while allowing others with different or opposing viewpoints to have their say without interruption or comment.

7. **Which of the following is not a right declared by the US Constitution?**
   (Average) (Skill 10.3)

   A.   The right to speak out in public

   B.   The right to use cruel and unusual punishment

   C.   The right to a speedy trial

   D.   The right not to be forced to testify against yourself

Answer: B. The right to use cruel and unusual punishment
A person who lives in a democratic society legally has a comprehensive list of rights guaranteed to him or her by the government. In the United States, this is the Constitution and its Amendments. Among these very important rights are:

- the right to speak out in public
- the right to pursue any religion
- the right for a group of people to gather in public for any reason that doesn't fall under a national security cloud
- the right not to have soldiers stationed in your home
- the right not to be forced to testify against yourself in a court of law
- the right to a speedy and public trial by a jury of your peers
- the right not to be the victim of cruel and unusual punishment
- the right to avoid unreasonable search and seizure of your person, your house, and your vehicle

8. **What group is most responsible for enforcing the law?**
   (Average) (Skill 10.3)

   A.   Executive Branch

   B.   Individual States

   C.   Judicial Branch

   D.   Legislative Branch

Answer: A. Executive Branch
The executive branch and its departments enforce federal laws. The Department of Justice, led by the United States Attorney General is the primary law enforcement department of the federal government. Other investigative and enforcement departments such as the Federal Bureau of Investigation (FBI) and the U.S. Postal Inspectors aid the Justice Department.

9. **Linguistics is which of the following?**
(Average) (Skill 10.4)

A.   Norms, values, standards

B.   Study of material remains of humans

C.   Genetic characteristics

D.   The historical development of language

Answer: D. The historical development of language
There are four areas of anthropology:

- archaeology: study of material remains of humans
- social-cultural: norms, values, standards
- biological: genetic characteristics
- linguistics: the historical development of language

10. **Which of the following refers to cultural influences?**
    (Average) (Skill 10.4)

    A.   General social patterns of groups of people in an area

    B.   Changes in attitudes, morale, and leadership

    C.   Organized groups of people

    D.   Wars, revolutions, inventions, and fashions

Answer: C. Organized groups of people
Sociology is the study of human society through the individuals, groups, and institutions that make up human society. Sociology includes every feature of human social conditions. It deals with the predominant behaviors, attitudes, and types of relationships within a society as defined by a group of people with a similar cultural background living in a specific geographical area. Sociology is divided into five major areas of study:

- Population studies: General social patterns of groups of people living in a certain geographical area.
- Social behaviors: Changes in attitudes, morale, leadership, conformity, and others.
- Social institutions: Organized groups of people performing specific functions within a society such as churches, schools, hospitals, business organizations, and governments.
- Cultural influences: Customs, knowledge, arts, religious beliefs, and language.
- Social change: Wars, revolutions, inventions, fashions, and other events or activities.

11. **Which of the following can be considered the primary goal of social studies?** *(Average) (Skill 10.5)*

   A.   Recalling specific dates and places

   B.   Identifying and analyzing social links

   C.   Using contextual clues to identify eras

   D.   Linking experiments with history

Answer: B. Identifying and analyzing social links
Historic events and social issues cannot be considered only in isolation. People and their actions are connected in many ways, and events are linked through cause and effect over time. Identifying and analyzing these social and historic links is a primary goal of the social sciences. The methods used to analyze social phenomena borrow from several of the social sciences. Interviews, statistical evaluation, observation, and experimentation are just some of the ways that people's opinions and motivations can be measured. From these opinions, larger social beliefs and movements can be interpreted, and events, issues and social problems can be placed in context to provide a fuller view of their importance.

Answer Key: Social Sciences

1.	D
2.	B
3.	B,
4.	C
5.	A
6.	D

7.	B
8.	A
9.	D
10.	C
11.	B

Rigor Table: Social Sciences

	Easy 36.4%	Average 54.5%	Rigorous 9.1%
Questions	1, 2, 3, 6,	5, 7, 8, 9, 10, 11	4

SOCIAL SCIENCES ESSAYS

You are an elementary school teacher at a Title 1 school. Your school district has been unable to purchase new textbooks for your school in several years. Because of that, the Social Studies textbooks in your classroom are becoming quickly out-dated and there are no supplemental materials to use for hands-on learning. Along with teaching the content Social Studies standards, you also have to be sure that your students are learning Historical and Social Science Analysis Skills which are often overlooked because of a lack of resources. These skills are not only an important aspect of creating independent thinkers in your classroom, they are also important to making Social Studies come alive for the students, to becoming relevant in their own lives. Being that you only have older Social Studies textbooks at your disposal and no additional resources in the classroom, you have to think "out of the box" to teach these analysis skills to your students.

Historical and Social Science Analysis Skills for grades K-5 include such ideas as:
- Chronological and Spatial Thinking
  - interpreting time lines
  - using terms related to time
  - connections between past and present
  - interpretation of maps and globes, and significance of location
- Research, Evidence, and Point of View
  - differentiation between primary and secondary sources
  - posing relevant questions about events and sources
  - distinguishing between fact and fiction
- Historical Interpretation
  - summarize key events and explain historical context of those events
  - identify human and physical characteristics of places and explain how these are unique to such places
  - identify and interpret multiple causes and effects of events

Given the above information and circumstance, create instructional strategies/activities to teach 2 to 3 of the Historical and Social Science Analysis Skills outlined above. These skills can be taught using any Social Studies content and are for grades K-5 as noted above.

Sample Response

The Historical and Social Science Analysis Skills can seem to be quite daunting to a classroom teacher, especially one with limited resources available. I understand, though, the importance of these skills in creating independent thinkers. I can also see how easily these skills can be brushed aside, leaving teachers to rely on and solely teach from a Social Studies textbook. I believe that Social Studies will only become relevant to students if these analysis skills are included in the teaching of the curriculum; they truly make the content come alive for the students. Considering that these skills are concurrent for grades K-5, it is important to start with simple, uncomplicated activities for the lower grades and then build to more complex activities for the upper grades. This idea is the basis of the activities described below.

For the analysis skill of distinguishing between fact and fiction:
- In Kindergarten, students learn about important historical legends and figures, such as Pocahontas and Benjamin Franklin. I will begin with reading to the students from the textbook. Then, as a class, we will discuss and make a list of why these figures are important. I will then read a fictional story about the figure to the class. We will then talk about the differences between the reading from the text and the fictional story. This will begin a continuing discussion between things that are fact and things that are fiction.
- In 2nd grade, students again learn about important historical figures and how they've made differences for us today. Similar activities can be used to review this analysis skill at the start of the school year. To further the students' understanding of this skill, another activity will involve a more hands on approach. The class will be divided into teams of 4. Each team will be assigned a historical figure from the textbook. They will then have to locate a storybook on that person in the library. The team will read aloud to the class information from the text and information from the storybook. On a T-chart, their classmates will write down what they believe to be factual information and fictional information. These T-charts will be shared with the class and the presenting team will lead a discussion regarding which information was factual and which was fictional.

For the analysis skill of making connections between the past and the present:
- In 1st grade, students study transportation methods of the past. To introduce this information, I will show students pictures of various modes of transportation throughout history. I will present these pictures in chronological order and lead a discussion of what life must have been like with these transportation methods. This will continue throughout the week as we reach more current methods of transportation. At the conclusion of this lesson, students will choose one of the modes of transportation and in a paragraph, write about how they think their life would have been like if that was the way their family got around. Then, the students will share their paragraphs with the class. We will then discuss how different life would be if we still used that

type of transportation. This series of lessons will conclude with a discussion of why changes have been made in transportation as time progressed.

- In 2nd grade, students compare/contrast their own lives with their parents and grandparents. To continue the study of making connections between the past and the present, students will begin the school year by creating a storyboard of their own life, including such things as clothes that are worn, modes of transportation, life at home, and life at school. This activity will be followed by creating a storyboard of the life of a grandparent or other elderly relative with the same categories. Students will then compare/contrast their storyboards. Choosing to either live as a child when their grandparent or relative did or to have their grandparent or relative be a child now, the students will write a story about what that life would be like, how it would be different. This series of activities will conclude with a class discussion about why some things have changed and some have not. These types of lessons could continue in 3rd grade when the students learn about the development of their communities.

One of the many great things about teaching the Historical and Social Sciences Analysis Skills is that they can so easily build upon each other and add depth to the content of textbooks. I believe that once a teacher begins to teach these skills in their classrooms, the skills become more easily integrated into everyday Social Studies lessons.

ARTS

1. **A student art sample book would include cotton balls and sandpaper to represent:**
    (Average) (Skill 13.1)

    A.   Color

    B.   Lines

    C.   Texture

    D.   Shape

Answer: C. Texture
Texture refers to the way something feels because of the tactile quality of its surface. An art sample book can include materials such as cotton balls and sandpaper as examples of different textures.

2. **Which terms refers to the arrangement of one or more items so they appear symmetrical or asymmetrical?**
    (Rigorous) (Skill 13.1)

    A.   Balance

    B.   Contrast

    C.   Emphasis

    D.   Unity

Answer: A. Balance
The principles of visual are that students should be introduced to include abstract, background, balance, contrast, emphasis, sketch, texture, and unity. Balance refers to the arrangement of one or more elements in a work of art so they appear symmetrical or asymmetrical in design and proportion

3. **Sound waves are produced by _____ .**
    (Easy) (Skill 13.2)

    A.   pitch

    B.   noise

    C.   vibrations

    D.   sonar

Answer: C. vibrations
Sound waves are produced by a vibrating body. The vibrating object moves forward and compresses the air in front of it, then reverses direction so that pressure on the air is lessened and expansion of the air molecules occurs. The vibrating air molecules move back and forth parallel to the direction of motion of the wave as they pass the energy from adjacent air molecules closer to the source to air molecules farther away from the source. Therefore, The correct answer is choice C.

4. **Common percussion instruments include:**
    (Average) (Skill 13.2)

    A.   Xylophone, tambourine, and bells

    B.   Trumpet, trombone, and tuba

    C.   Oboe, clarinet, and saxophone

    D.   Viola, cello, and piano

Answer: A. Xylophone, tambourine, and bells
Percussion instruments are those that the musician hits or shakes to make sound. These include the xylophone, tambourine, and bells. Both brass and wind instruments make sound as air travels through an air chamber. Trumpets, trombones, and tubas are examples of brass instruments and the oboe, clarinet and saxophone are examples of wind instruments. The viola, cello, and piano are examples of string instruments.

5. **A combination of three or more tones sounded at the same time is called a:** *(Average) (Skill 13.2)*

    A.   Harmony

    B.   Consonance

    C.   Chord

    D.   Dissonance

Answer: C. Chord
This is a musical definition of a chord that should be learned from your program of study.

6. **A series of single tones which add up to a recognizable sound is called a:** *(Average) (Skill 13.2)*

    A.   Cadence

    B.   Rhythm

    C.   Melody

    D.   Sequence

Answer: C. Melody
This is a musical definition of a melody that should be learned from your program of study.

7. **The quality of sound is the definition of:**
   (Average) (Skill 13.2)

   A.   Timbre

   B.   Rhythm

   C.   Harmony

   D.   Melody

Answer: A. Timbre
Rhythm refers to the duration of musical notes. Harmony refers to the vertical aspect of music or the musical chords related to a melody. Finally, melody is the tune (a specific arrangement of sounds in a pleasing pattern).

8. **In visual arts such as music and dance, the intentional, regular repetition of a given element most commonly serves as a feeling of:**
   (Average) (Skill 14.1)

   A.   Rhythm

   B.   Dissonance

   C.   Contrast

   D.   Dominance

Answer: A. Rhythm
Rhythm is the basis of dance and is developed through repetition and practice.

9. **In visual art studies students are expected to be able to interact in all of the following exercises EXCEPT one.**
    (Average) (Skill 14.1)

    A.   Clap out rhythmic patterns found in music lyrics

    B.   Compare and contrast various art pieces

    C.   Recognize related dance vocabulary

    D.   Identify and sort pictures organized by shape, size, and color

Answer: C. Recognize related dance vocabulary
Dance is not a related area in visual arts.

10. **Creating movements in response to music helps students to connect music and dance in which of the following ways?**
    (Average) (Skill 14.1)

    A.   Rhythm

    B.   Costuming

    C.   Speed

    D.   Vocabulary skills

Answer: A. Rhythm
Students should be able to understand the connections made between movement and music is related by rhythm.

11. **Which subject would a color wheel most likely be used for?**
    (Easy) (Skill 14.1)

    A.   Visual arts

    B.   Music

    C.   Movement

    D.   Drama

Answer: A. Visual arts
A color wheel is an important tool in teaching students visual arts. It is used to teach students about primary and secondary colors. It is also used to help students learn about mixing colors.

12. **What would watching a dance company performance be most likely to promote?**
    (Easy) (Skill 14.1)

    A.   Critical thinking skills

    B.   Appreciation of the arts

    C.   Improvisation skills

    D.   Music vocabulary

Answer: B. Appreciation of the arts
Live performances are an important part of learning arts and help to develop aesthetic appreciation of the arts. A dance company performance is one example of a live performance that students could attend.

Answer Key: Arts

1.	C	7.	A
2.	A	8.	A
3.	C	9.	C
4.	A	10.	A
5.	C	11.	A
6.	C	12.	B

Rigor Table: Arts

	Easy 25%	Average 66.7%	Rigorous 8.3%
Questions	3, 11, 12	1, 4, 5, 6, 7, 8, 9, 10	3

CPSIA information can be obtained at www.ICGtesting.com
Printed in the USA
LVOW031613200412

278500LV00002B/31/P

WITHDRAWAL

9 781607 871170